egg carton critters

egg carton

Photographs by Robert L. Dunne

critters

Created by Donna Miller

Scholastic Book Services

New York   Toronto   London   Auckland   Sydney   Tokyo

Text and Illustrations Copyright © 1978
by Robert L. Dunne and Donna Sterman.
All rights reserved.
This edition is published by
Scholastic Book Services, a division of
Scholastic Magazines, Inc., 50 West 44th Street,
New York, N.Y. 10036, by arrangement with
Walker Publishing Company, Inc.

12 11 10 9 8 7 6 5 4 3 2   9/7 0 1 2 3 4/8
                Printed in the U.S.A.   02

There is a whole world of critters waiting to be discovered in an egg carton.

Egg carton critters are a lot of fun to make. They can be used as party and holiday decorations or given to family and friends as presents. Some of the critters will work as puppets. All of them look great hung on a wall or from the ceiling of your room. You'll also be recycling something that usually ends up in the trash.

We hope you will enjoy making the critters in this book as well as creating some new ones of your own.

Here are the **materials** you will need.

1. Cardboard egg cartons — get the ones with flat solid lids
2. Assorted colored construction paper
3. Poster or acrylic paints
4. Paint brushes
5. Scissors
6. Rubber bands
7. White glue
8. Masking tape
9. Stapler — optional
10. Pipe cleaners or twist 'ems
11. Paper fasteners — for hand puppets

Hints on gluing — Put glue on both pieces that you want to stick together. Use rubber bands to hold the pieces in place until they are dry. Be patient and don't try to paint your critters until all the glue has dried.

Hints on painting — Use your biggest paint brush and have your paint thick rather than watery. Light colored critters may take several coats of paint to cover the lettering that is on most cartons. Let each coat dry before putting on another.

Look at the pictures and pick out the critter you want to make. There is an index on page 32 which will tell you where to find the directions for making each critter.

Caterpillar

Ant

Sea Turtle

Caterpillar

BODY — Cut out six connected egg cups and trim off about 1/4 inch from the edges of the cups. This will make the top of the caterpillar. Cut out the other six connected egg cups and then cut one of them off to use for a mouth.

Trim 1/2 inch off the edges of the five egg cups, leaving just enough of the carton in between cups to hold them together. This will make the bottom of the caterpillar. Glue the bottom inside the top.

HEAD — Glue the mouth cup inside the last body cup for the head.

FEELERS — Curl pipe cleaners or cut strips of paper and curl them around a pencil.

Ant

Follow the steps for making the caterpillar but use three egg cups instead of six.

Add pipe cleaners or twist 'ems for legs and feelers.

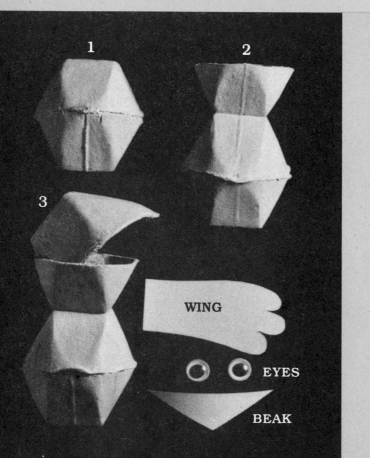

Baby Birds

BODY — Cut out two egg cups. Trim them until the edges are even and then glue them together (1).

HEAD — Glue a third egg cup on top of the body (2). Trim a fourth egg cup to a point on one side. Glue it inside the third egg cup (3).

WINGS, EYES — Cut out of construction paper; or you can use plastic wiggly eyes from a sewing notion store.

You can find the picture of baby birds on page one.

10

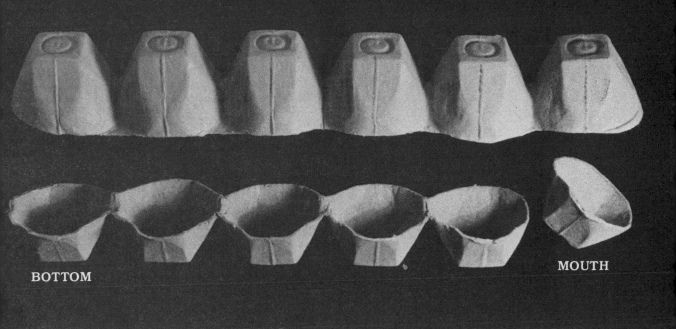

BOTTOM

MOUTH

Sea Turtle

BODY — Cut out four connected egg cups to make the top. Cut off the points.

Cut out another four cups to make the bottom and cut off the points. Without separating the egg cups, trim off 1/2 inch from the edges of the cups.

Tape or glue the bottom inside the top (as shown).

HEAD — Use two egg cups to make a top and bottom. Cut off bottom cup smaller than the top one. Glue or staple it at an angle inside the top cup.

Tape or glue the head to the body.

EYES, TOES, TAIL — Cut out of construction paper.

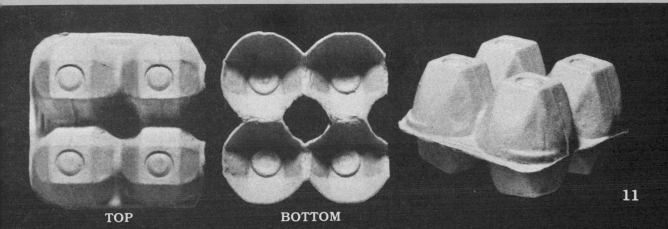

TOP

BOTTOM

Rabbit

Rabbit

BODY—For the main part of the body use two lids. Trim off the bottom edges evenly. Use tape to hold the two lids together. Trim the bottom again if the critter doesn't stand straight.

Then cut another lid in half and trim the two bottoms. Cut away one side of each half lid and cut a notch out of the top as shown by the dotted lines. Fit the pieces snugly against the side of the tall part of the body.

Glue or tape the half lids together and then glue them to the body.

HEAD—Cut off a piece of lid the length that you want the critter's head to be. Staple or glue it to the front of the body.

EYES—Cut out two cups from the carton. Cut off the point. Trim the edges of each cup evenly and glue to the top of the head.

EARS—Cut out the ears from the sides of a half lid and slip in between the two halves of the head, then glue or tape together.

WHISKERS, TAIL—Broom straws make good whiskers while a pom-pom or cotton ball works well as a tail.

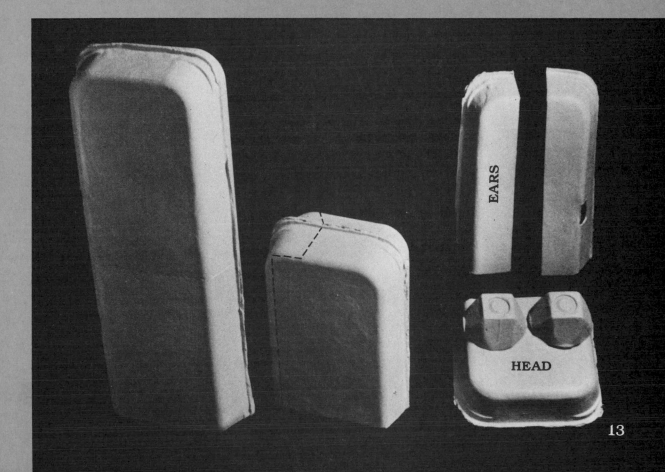

EARS

HEAD

13

Finger Puppets

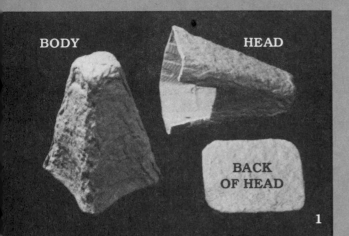

BODY   HEAD

BACK
OF HEAD

1

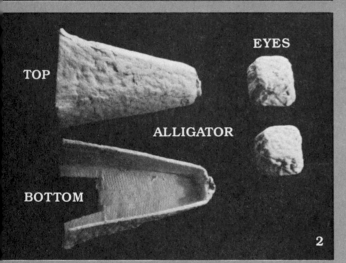

TOP

EYES

ALLIGATOR

BOTTOM

2

3

Finger Puppets

All of them are made from the points from inside the egg carton.

HEAD—Cut one point from the carton for the head. If you want to make a short head, rather than a regular one, cut more off the bottom of the point.

Trim the bottom evenly. Trace around the bottom of the head on a scrap of lid.

Cut out this back piece. Cut a small square out of the head as shown in photo 1.

For the *alligator's* head (photo 2) cut the point in half. Use one half for the top and the other for the bottom.

Glue the bottom inside the top. Cut the tips off two points for eyes.

BODY—Cut out another point from the carton and trim its bottom evenly.

PUT IT TOGETHER—Slide the head over the body (photo 3) and glue or tape in place. Then glue the back onto the head.

Cut ears and horns from lid scraps or colored paper and glue on. Broom straws make good whiskers. Use "wiggly" eyes from a sewing notion store or cut out of construction paper.

Frog

Penguins

Owl

Raccoon

Giraffe

OPOSSUM

Martian Mobiles

Frog, Penguins, Owl, Raccoon, Giraffe, Martians

BODY—All of these critters can be made either short or tall. For short ones begin with two half lids. Tall critters need two whole lids. Glue the two lids together. Trim off the bottom edges evenly so that the critter will stand straight.

HEAD—Only the *frog* and *giraffe* need special heads. Cut off a piece of lid the length that you want the critter's head to be. Staple or glue it at an angle to the front of the body as shown below.

BUGGY EYES — Every critter but the penguin and opossum needs buggy eyes. Cut out two cups from the carton. Trim the edges of each cup evenly. Glue the cups to the head and paint in the eyes.

PENGUIN EYES — From the bottom of the carton, cut out in one piece two cups with a point between them. Then cut away about half the sides of the cups. Cut the carton's point to look like the penguin's bill.

FEET, EARS, WINGS, LEGS, HORNS and other parts — Can be cut from scraps of the lid, cups, points or construction paper.

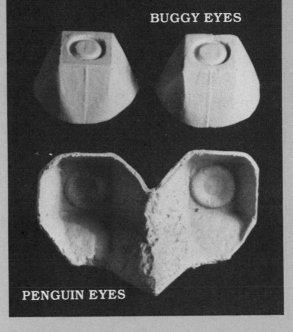

Opossum

BODY — Cut a lid in half. Slide one half inside the other and glue together.

HEAD — Cut out in one piece, from the bottom of the carton, two cups with a point between them. Cut away about half the sides of the cups.
Then glue this piece to the bottom of the body. Paint the circles in the eyes or cut out of colored paper.

FEET, EARS — Cut out pieces from lid scraps. Use the corners of the lid for the ears.

TAIL — Made from yarn or cording.

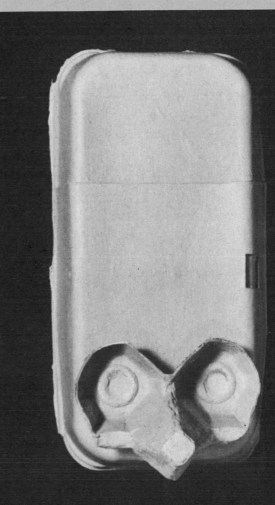

27

Dragon

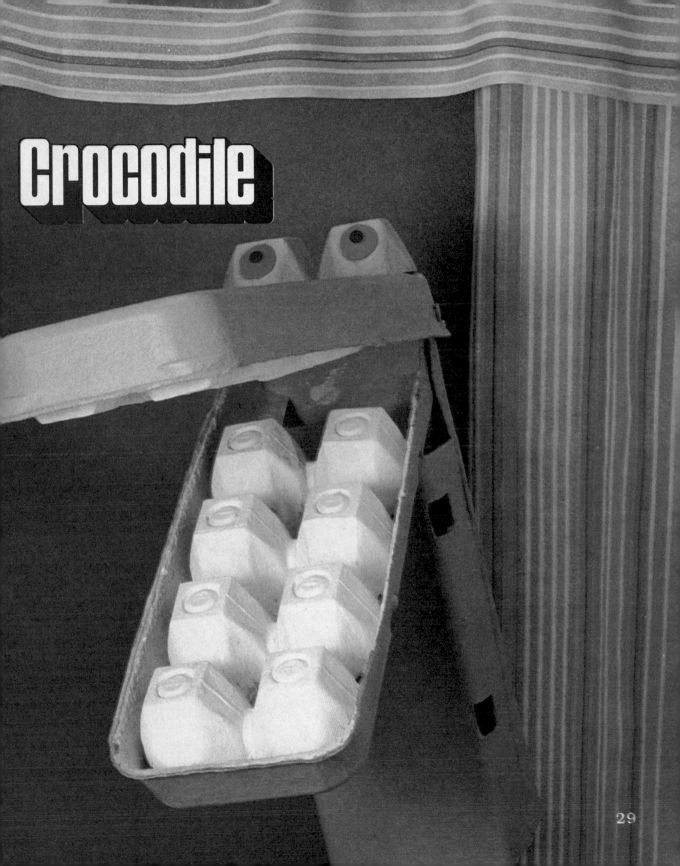

Crocodile

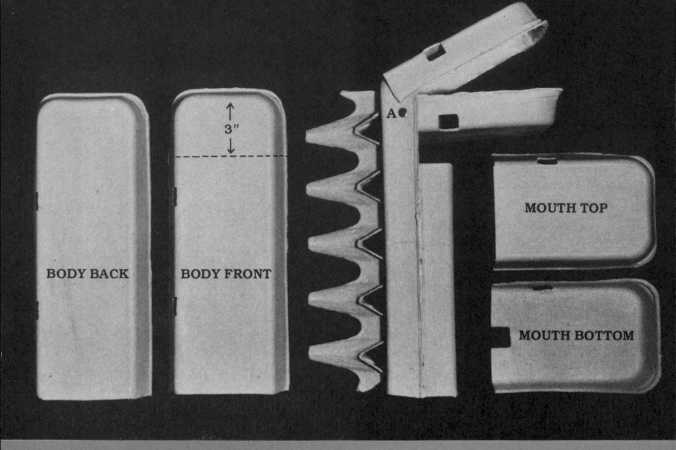

BODY BACK · BODY FRONT · 3" · A · MOUTH TOP · MOUTH BOTTOM

Dragon Puppet

MOUTH—Cut a lid in half. Use one half for the top and the other to make the bottom.
From the bottom half, cut out a notch big enough for one finger to fit.

BODY—Cut off the bottom ends of two lids. One will be the front and the other the back.
Cut three inches off the top and sides of the front lid piece (see dotted line).

PUT IT TOGETHER—Staple and glue the mouth top to the body back. Make a small hole at A and attach the mouth bottom with a paper fastener or twist 'em. Repeat on the other side.
Glue or tape the body front to the back.
Add egg cups for eyes. Cut away the sides of a carton bottom leaving a strip of points for spines.

TO OPERATE—Slide your hand inside the body and put a finger in the notch of the mouth bottom. Pull gently and the mouth will move.

Crocodile Puppet

MOUTH—Use two lids for a top and bottom. Cut off one end of the bottom lid as shown.

TEETH—Use eight egg cups all in one piece. Trim 1/2 inch off all around the cups and cut off the three points. Repeat so that you have two sets of teeth.

BODY—Make the body from two lids. Cut the bottom ends from both lids. Draw a line around the front piece 2 1/2 inches from the top. Cut along this line.

PUT IT TOGETHER—Glue the teeth inside the top and bottom of the mouth.
Attach the mouth top to the body back by making a small hole at B. Put in a paper fastener or twist'em. Repeat on the other side.
Staple and glue the mouth bottom under the top.
Glue or tape the body front to the back. Add egg cups for eyes.

TO OPERATE—Slide your hand through the hole in the mouth bottom and lift up the top of the mouth.

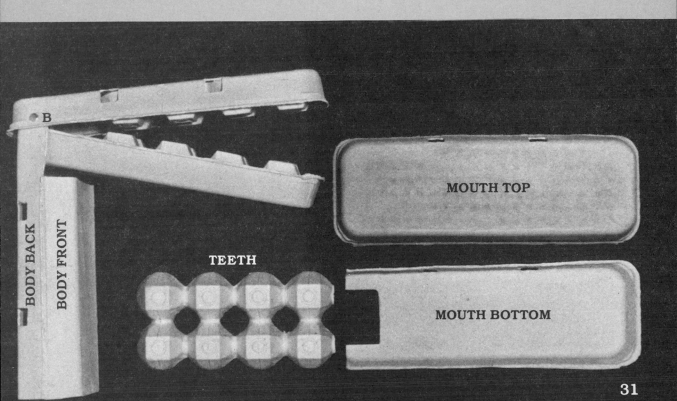

B

BODY BACK

BODY FRONT

TEETH

MOUTH TOP

MOUTH BOTTOM

INDEX

CRITTER